THE HIP-HOP REVOLUTION

JAY-Z

EXCELLING IN MUSIC AND BUSINESS

EILEEN LUCAS

Enslow Publishing
101 W. 23rd Street
Suite 240
New York, NY 10011
USA

enslow.com

Published in 2020 by Enslow Publishing, LLC.
101 W. 23rd Street, Suite 240, New York, NY 10011

Library of Congress Cataloging-in-Publication Data

Names: Lucas, Eileen, author.
Title: Jay-Z : excelling in music and business / Eileen Lucas.
Description: New York : Enslow Publishing, 2020. | Series: The hip-hop revolution | Audience: 5 | Includes bibliographical references and index.
Identifiers: LCCN 2018048704| ISBN 9781978509665 (library bound) | ISBN 9781978510173 (pbk.) | ISBN 9781978510197 (6 pack)
Subjects: LCSH: Jay-Z, 1969—Juvenile literature. | Rap musicians—United States—Biography—Juvenile literature.
Classification: LCC ML3930.J38 L83 2020 | DDC 782.421649092 [B] —dc23
LC record available at https://lccn.loc.gov/2018048704

Printed in the United States of America

To Our Readers: We have done our best to make sure all websites in this book were active and appropriate when we went to press. However, the author and the publisher have no control over and assume no liability for the material available on those websites or on any websites they may link to. Any comments or suggestions can be sent by email to customerservice@enslow.com.

Photo Credits: Cover, p. 1 Kevin Mazur/Getty Images; pp. 5, 17 Johnny Nunez/WireImage/Getty Images; p. 7 Jamie McCarthy/WireImage/Getty Images; p. 8 Al Pereira/Michael Ochs Archives/Getty Images; pp. 11; 14 Sylvain Gaboury/FilmMagic/Getty Images; p. 13 Chris Walter/WireImage/Getty Images; p. 18 © AP Images; p. 20 Scott Gries/Getty Images; p. 23 James Devaney/WireImage/Getty Images; p. 24 Theo Wargo/Getty Images; p. 26 John Ricard/Getty Images; title graphics (arrows) Vecster/Shutterstock.com.

CONTENTS

COMING FROM NOTHING

S hawn swung a leg over the big two-wheeled bike. The neighbors watched in amazement as the four-year-old powered it down the street. Shawn later called the experience his first taste of being famous. "I liked it," he said. "Felt good."[1]

Shawn Corey Carter was born December 4, 1968. He grew up in the Brooklyn area of New York City. His family lived in an apartment that was part of the Marcy Projects. The projects were filled with people who struggled every day, and with those who'd lost hope. The neighborhood was plagued with drugs and violence. It would take a great deal of toughness and hard work to escape. But Shawn eventually did escape. He would become famous and wealthy as Jay-Z, rapper and hip-hop businessman.

Jay-Z attends the premiere of a video game he produced called *NBA 2K13* at his 40/40 Club in New York City, on September 26, 2012. His success extends beyond the music industry.

A GIFTED CHILD

Shawn had a few things going for him that not everyone had. He was a bright student and loved to read. He had a loving, hard-working mother in Gloria Carter. He felt especially close to his sister Andrea, who he called Annie. Another sister, Mickey, and a brother, Eric, completed the family. Shawn's father, Adnis Reeves, left home when Shawn was young. Shawn grew up feeling hurt and angry without a dad.

The Marcy Projects

Jay-Z grew up in a tough neighborhood in New York City. The apartment he lived in was part of what is called "public housing," or "a project." The projects were built for people who are too poor to live anywhere else. Jay-Z would describe how dangerous Marcy was in many of his songs.

Shawn was alone a lot as he grew up. One thing he loved doing was thinking of rhymes. He had a notebook that he filled with them. Sometimes he wrote them down on scraps of paper. Later, he'd pull them from his pockets. He'd often wake the family up at night. They'd find him tapping out a beat on the kitchen table.

SURVIVING THE STREET LIFE

Gloria did her best to raise the children and pay the bills. But she had to work a lot. As a teenager, Shawn turned to the streets. There he found the only opportunity he could see for earning money—selling drugs.

This was the height of the crack epidemic in America. Shawn saw the terrible effects of this and other drugs on people. He chose not to do drugs himself. But making money selling them became his job.

Jay-Z remains close to his mother, Gloria Carter, and she supports his work. Here, they raise money at a Shawn Carter Foundation event in 2011.

It was a dangerous way of life. Weapons were all around. Shawn lived in fear of being beaten or killed, or going to jail.

Then Shawn became friends with Jaz-O, a rapper from the Marcy Projects. Shawn wondered if rapping might bring him a better life. He'd sometimes been

A young Jay-Z (*right*) is shown with two of the many hip-hop artists he has worked with, Jaz-O (*left*) and Queen Latifah.

called "jazzy" as a kid. With a nod to his friend Jaz-O, he adopted Jay-Z as his rap name.

RAPPING ON THE SPOT

Jay-Z continued to pour his hopes and dreams into rhymes. He went to parties and took over the microphone as often as he could. He emceed in contests around the projects. Emcees (or MCs) were the ones who spoke into microphones. They did this while DJs spun the beats on turntables. He became known as a "freestyler." This meant he could make up rhymes on the spot. All the years of writing down rhymes was paying off.

"All I got is dreams, nobody else can see. Nobody else believes, nobody else but me."[2]

He told those that would listen of his dreams of making it in hip-hop. He said his goal as a rapper was to "have a conversation with the world." He planned to "speak about the people and the neighborhoods" he'd come from. He'd show what "someone who comes from nothing" had to say.[3]

FIVE YEARS, FIVE ALBUMS

A big step in Jay-Z's escape from the projects came when he met Damon Dash. Dash came from the East Harlem part of New York City. Like Jay-Z, he was very interested in the music and life of hip-hop. In 1995, "Dam" and "J" started their own recording company. Dash mostly ran the business side of Roc-A-Fella Records. Jay-Z took the lead on creating rhymes and beats. Together they found some office space and got to work.

It could be difficult to get anyone to pay attention at first. Sometimes they sold music out of the trunk of a car. In 1996, they recorded Jay-Z's first album, *Reasonable Doubt*. On it, Jay-Z rhymed about the streets that he knew. "Reflecting the truth of our lives," he called it.[1] *Rolling Stone* magazine later listed it as one of the five hundred greatest albums of all time.

In 2002, Jay-Z helps celebrate his Roc-A-Fella partner Damon Dash's birthday at a party in the hometown they share, New York City.

ONE OF THE RAP GREATS

A rapper from the same part of town as Jay-Z performed on the album. Christopher Wallace had even gone to one of the same schools as Jay-Z. Now he was known as the Notorious B.I.G., Biggie Smalls, or just Biggie. He and Jay-Z had become friends. Sadly, in March 1997, Biggie was shot and killed in Los Angeles. Just a few months before, rapper Tupac Shakur had been shot to death in Las Vegas.

Meaningful Rhymes

For Jay-Z, rap was part reporting, part entertainment, and part art. All parts mattered to him. He used words as metaphors to create images in listeners' heads, especially those who'd grown up like him in a world that felt like a war zone. There were always many layers of meaning in his rhymes.

Jay-Z's second album, released in 1997, was called *In My Lifetime, Vol. 1.* Jay-Z would later call this one of the worst periods of his life. Besides the death of his friend, there was conflict between the East Coast and West Coast worlds of hip-hop. Still, the album sold even better than Jay-Z's first album had.

By this time, Roc-A-Fella was working with a company called Def Jam Records. Def Jam was a big deal in the hip-hop world. It could help get some attention for Jay-Z's rhymes.

Jay-Z's next album, *Vol.2...Hard Knock Life,* was one of his most successful works. It won a Grammy Award, but Jay-Z did not attend the ceremony. He thought other rappers were not getting enough attention. *Rolling Stone* magazine named Jay-Z the Best Hip-Hop Artist of 1998.

The Notorious B.I.G. performs in 1995. No one was ever charged for killing Biggie at the age of twenty-four.

Jay-Z signs autographs at a 2003 event in a Bloomingdale's clothing store while wearing a Rocawear shirt. Rocawear has become a multimillion-dollar company.

GOING INTO FASHION

In 1999, Jay-Z released *Vol.3 . . . Life and Times of S. Carter*. The album after that was called *The Dynasty: Roc La Familia*. This was his fifth album in five years. At the same time, Jay-Z was moving into other areas of hip-hop business. He and Roc-A-Fella partner Damon Dash started a clothing line called Rocawear. Jay-Z promoted the line by wearing some of the clothes onstage.

Then Jay-Z learned how quickly he could lose all the success he'd gained. He was trying to stop bootlegging, or stealing music over the internet. He'd had an argument with record producer Lance Rivera. At a party one night, Jay-Z lost control. He stabbed Rivera in the stomach. Fortunately, Rivera was not seriously hurt. In 2001, Jay-Z served three years probation for the attack. After this, he promised himself he would never get into that kind of trouble again.

> "I did bad things [in the past] . . . I try not to do bad things anymore."[2]

FORGIVING THE PAST

Jay-Z's sixth album was due for release on September 11, 2001. No one expected that there would be a terrorist attack on the United States that day. In time, however, *The Blueprint* continued Jay-Z's history of success.

Jay-Z's next album, *The Blueprint 2: The Gift & the Curse,* included a single titled "03 Bonnie & Clyde." It featured well-known singer Beyoncé Knowles. When she released her first solo album in 2003, it included a song called "Crazy in Love." This song featured Jay-Z. The performers sang the song together at the MTV Music Awards that year. They did not immediately make it public that they were dating.

On Jay-Z's *The Black Album*, his mom, Gloria Carter, can be heard speaking. He had recorded her voice while she was talking in the studio one day.

Jay-Z continued to expand his influence in hip-hop. He participated in a number of tours and festivals. Some concert promoters had feared that hip-hop concerts would become violent. With his successful events, Jay-Z helped open doors for other rappers.

Jay-Z also opened the doors of his first 40/40 Club in New York. Over time, many famous athletes and other stars enjoyed spending time at his sports bars.

Business partner Damon Dash was on hand to help Jay-Z celebrate the opening of the first 40/40 Club in New York City in 2003.

RETIRING FROM RAP

About this time, there were rumors that Jay-Z was going to take a break from rapping. On November 25, 2003, he held a concert at Madison Square Garden. He called it a "retirement party." It opened with an announcer saying, "The one, the only, champion of the world of hip-hop, Jay-Z!"[1] It closed with a giant jersey with his name on it lifted to the roof. Beyoncé and other artists

Jay-Z called his Madison Square Garden concert in 2003 a "retirement party," but it definitely wasn't the end of his hip-hop career.

performed at this concert. All the money raised was given to charity.

While Jay-Z did take some time off from making new studio albums in "retirement," he didn't really leave the business. In 2004, he was named president of Def Jam records. This was the same company Roc-A-Fella Records had worked with at the start of Jay-Z's career. Def Jam had purchased Roc-A-Fella. As president, Jay-Z could play a part in helping other performers get started.

NO MORE ANGER

Jay-Z also had a chance to meet with his dad before he died in 2003. "Me and my pop got to talk," Jay-Z would

Hip-Hop Won't Stop

In 2006, the Smithsonian Institution and the National Museum of American History planned to create a major exhibit about hip-hop. It would include items from the earliest rappers to the current stars. This is proof that hip-hop has reached beyond the inner city. It has become an important part of American culture.

Fans were pleased when Jay-Z and Nas performed onstage together in East Rutherford, New Jersey, in October, 2005, ending their "war of words."

later tell *Rolling Stone*. "I got to tell him everything I wanted to say."[2] In one of his songs, Jay-Z would tell his dad that he'd forgiven him for leaving the family long ago.

On October 27, 2005, Jay-Z headlined a concert called "I Declare War." Fans wondered whom Jay-Z was declaring war on! At the end of the concert, he brought another rapper on-stage. It was Nas, someone with whom he had exchanged angry words. The two had even rapped insults at each other. To the crowd's delight, the two rappers shook hands onstage. Then they performed a blend of Jay-Z's and Nas's songs. They had worked out their differences without going to war.

In 2007, Jay-Z's tenth album, *American Gangster*, sold one million copies in the United States alone. The following year, he left his position as president of Def Jam Records. Once again, he was ready to expand in a new direction.

"Rappers took the noise of urban life and turned it into music."[3]

A LONG WAY FROM MARCY

Rappers often speak out about the struggles of people around them. Many want to do more to change things. Jay-Z often supports various "Get Out the Vote" campaigns. This is a way for the "invisible people" to let their voices be heard. In 2006, Jay-Z worked with the United Nations to raise awareness of global water shortages.

A GROWING FAMILY

In April of 2008, Jay-Z married Beyoncé Knowles. The two had been quietly dating for some time. The wedding was held in Jay-Z's New York City apartment. Only close family and friends were invited. A friend says they are both "very down-to-earth" in real life. They are also very private people. They would rather have their work

Jay-Z and Beyoncé Knowles enjoy a basketball game at Madison Square Garden while dating in 2005.

than their personal life in the news. When they go out to dinner, they are "Mr. and Mrs. Carter."

Their first child was born in 2012. Newborn Blue Ivy Carter can be heard crying on one of Jay-Z's songs. When the song hit the Billboard charts, Blue Ivy became the youngest person to appear on a Billboard-charted song.

Mr. and Mrs. Carter and their daughter Blue Ivy are among the celebrities attending the NBA All-Star Game in New Orleans on February 19, 2017.

In spring of 2013, Jay-Z began a sports agency, Roc Nation Sports. It was part of Jay-Z's larger company, Roc Nation. Roc Nation Sports would soon be acting as agent for a number of well-known athletes.

In June 2017, Beyoncé and Jay-Z became parents of twins. The Carters named their daughter Rumi and her twin brother Sir.

In today's age of music streaming, Jay-Z works with a service called Tidal. A project titled *4:44* was released in 2017 to customers of Tidal and an internet service provider. Later, the album was made available on other platforms.

On June 6, 2018, Jay-Z and Beyoncé kicked off a new tour in the United Kingdom. Ten days later, they released a joint studio album, titled *Everything Is Love*. The album's credits list the performers as "The Carters."

GIVING BACK TO THE COMMUNITY

Jay-Z has rapped that the greatest form of giving is to remain anonymous. That said, in 2003, Jay-Z and

The Rapper Talks Books with Oprah

Jay-Z has always been a fan of reading. He has shared lists of books that have had an impact on his life. Once, at a dinner party in New York, he discussed this with fellow book lover and talk show host Oprah Winfrey. They might not share an appreciation for rap, but she did gain respect for the rapper.

his mom founded the Shawn Carter Foundation. This organization helps students who couldn't otherwise attend college. After Hurricane Katrina in 2005, he promised to give a million dollars to relief efforts. He has performed many times with Bono, the lead singer of U2, and other stars in support of worthwhile causes. In August 2018, Jay-Z and Beyoncé announced that they were giving more than a million dollars in scholarships to students. They would work with the Boys and Girls Clubs of America to choose the winners.

Jay-Z often collaborates with other hip-hop artists. Here he is shown with rapper Sean "Diddy" Combs at a 2005 charity event.

Jay-Z ranks among the most successful music artists of all time. His albums have sold more than fifty million copies around the world. He has received many awards, including twenty-one Grammys. He has had fourteen number one albums on the Billboard 200. He is a successful businessman and is devoted to his family. He has come a long way from the Marcy Projects.

"Every human being has genius-level talent. . . . You just have to find what it is that you are great at, and then tap into it."[1]

TIMELINE

1968 Shawn Corey Carter is born on December 4 in New York City.

1995 Jay-Z, Damon Dash, and a third partner form Roc-A-Fella Records.

1996 Jay-Z's first album, *Reasonable Doubt*, is recorded.

2000 Jay-Z and Damon Dash open the Rocawear clothing company.

2003 Jay-Z opens his first 40/40 Club in New York City. Jay-Z holds a "retirement party" concert on November 25 in Madison Square Garden, in New York.

2004 Jay-Z becomes president of Def Jam Records, an office he holds for four years.

2008 Jay-Z marries Beyoncé Knowles on April 4.

2012 Blue Ivy Carter is born on January 7.

2013 Jay-Z becomes a sports agent through his company Roc Nation Sports.

2017 Twins, Rumi and Sir Carter, are born on June 13.

2018 The Carters kick off a tour in the United Kingdom and release a joint studio album called *Everything Is Love*.

CHAPTER NOTES

CHAPTER 1. COMING FROM NOTHING

1. Jake Brown, *Jay-Z and the Roc-A-Fella Records Dynasty* (Phoenix, AZ: Amber Books, 2006), p. 6.

2. Ibid., pp. 32–33.

3. Lyrics to "History" by Jay-Z, in *Empire State of Mind, How Jay-Z Went from Street Corner to Corner Office* by Zack O'Malley Greenburg (New York, NY: Penguin/Portfolio, 2011), p. 205.

CHAPTER 2. FIVE YEARS, FIVE ALBUMS

1. Jay-Z, *Decoded* (New York, NY: Spiegel & Grau, 2011), p. 16.

2. Jake Brown, *Jay-Z and the Roc-A-Fella Records Dynasty* (Phoenix, AZ: Amber Books, 2006), p. 155.

CHAPTER 3. FORGIVING THE PAST

1. Zack O'Malley Greenburg, *Empire State of Mind, How Jay-Z Went from Street Corner to Corner Office* (New York, NY: Penguin/Portfolio, 2011), p. 84.

2. Ibid., p. 95.

3. Jay-Z, *Decoded* (New York, NY: Spiegel & Grau, 2011), p. 255.

CHAPTER 4. A LONG WAY FROM MARCY

1. Hardwood Highlight, "Jay-Z - Inspirational That Everyone Is a Genius," YouTube, January 2, 2015, https://www.youtube.com/watch?v=ydsmqw_6YQE.

GLOSSARY

agency A company that represents an athlete or a person in the entertainment industry.

blueprint A drawing that shows the plan for how something will be made or built.

bootlegging The sale of something taken or received illegally.

campaign A series of events supporting a cause.

epidemic A widespread problem.

freestyler A rapper who makes up words off the top of their head.

inner city The part of a city where the poorest people live.

probation A period of time when someone who has committed a crime has to behave and check in with an officer instead of going to jail.

shortage Not having enough of something, such as water.

streaming A way to send or receive video or sound files over a computer in a steady flow.

urban Having to do with large cities.

FURTHER READING

BOOKS

Bookout, Summer. *Jay-Z*. Broomall, PA : Mason Crest, 2018.

Cummings, Judy Dodge. *The Men of Hip-Hop*. Minneapolis, MN: Essential Library, 2018.

Kampff, Joseph. *Jay Z: Rapper and Businessman*. New York, NY: Enslow Publishing, 2016.

Oswald, Vanessa. *Jay-Z: Building a Hip-hop Empire*. New York, NY: Lucent Press, 2019.

WEBSITES

Jay-Z's Life + Times
lifeandtimes.com
Explore Jay-Z's official website, which includes information on music, fashion, sports, and other projects.

Kidzworld
www.kidzworld.com/article/5321-pioneers-of-hip-hop
Read about how hip-hop and rap got started.

The Shawn Carter Foundation
www.shawncartersf.com
Find out more about Jay-Z's organization, which helps low-income students attend college.

INDEX